The
MANY LESSONS
LEARNED SO FAR

The MANY LESSONS LEARNED SO FAR

Amanda Exantus

Library of Congress Control Number: 2012903908
ISBN: Hardcover   978-1-4691-7765-6
                Softcover   978-1-4691-7764-9
                Ebook   978-1-4691-7766-3

This book was printed in the United States of America.

To order additional copies of this book, contact:
Xlibris Corporation
1-888-795-4274
www.Xlibris.com
Orders@Xlibris.com
104397

Contents

I want to dedicate this publication to my parents, whom I love dearly. I am here today and am able to express my thoughts because of them and their sacrifices. I am forever grateful and thankful for their dedication and willingness to offer their children the best of this world. Thank you for the support and love. I love you, Mommy and Papi.

BIOGRAPHY

AMANDA EXANTUS HAS always shared a passion to speak into the lives of young ones and be a blessing and a light in any way that she can. Born and raised in Port-au-Prince, Haiti, she grew up in a loving family consisting of both parents, her brother, sister and surrounded by wonderful family members. She was given the opportunity to travel and pursue her education in the United States. During her stay, she encountered many individuals who, in some way or another, poured wisdom in her life. Her biggest dream is to go back home to be an asset and a positive voice in the upbringing of the youngsters of her country. After the tragic earthquake Haiti had faced on January 12, 2010, she perceived the catastrophe as an incentive to achieve her goal. Along with her faith in God, she is confident she will see the day when her country will offer hope and opportunities to the youth and guide and help them to live to the best of their abilities.

PREFACE

*T*HE MANY LESSONS *Learned So Far* contains many insights, examinations, and reservations I have had after I graduated from high school and as I was getting ready to take my first step into adulthood. I was very hesitant about enrolling in college, and choosing a career to specialize in is one of the most important decisions any of us has to make. Therefore, I was wrestling back and forth with different questions, such as, "What should my major be? What should I expect from these four years? Will I be able to balance everything?"

This book consists of different thoughts and realization that I have come to embrace during my college experience. Being an international student, I walked into the situation with a view that I have obtained from watching movies, reality shows and hearing my friends' personal experiences. I was highly shocked in my freshman year and had to quickly adjust.

I decided to write the reality I have learned and faced, for I felt compelled to not let my fellow companions march into the situation as blind and clueless as I was. *The Many Lessons Learned So Far* will hopefully help you attain a fresh perspective on the areas in which you might have to face in the future. The selected topics address the diffrent issues my friends and I underwent and the outcomes and conclusions we drew out of them.

After four years of reflecting, conversing with classmates, sharing experiences, attending classes, and journaling, I have put my all in condensing everything into this book. I sincerely hope the purpose behind this realization is met, and that is to help all who wonder about what comes after or what to expect.

THE IMPORTANCE OF EDUCATION

Education is for improving the lives of others and for leaving your community and world better than you found it.

—Marian Wright Edelman

Education is not a product: mark, diploma, job, money in that order; it is a process, a never ending one.

—Bel Kaufman

I REMEMBER, GROWING up, education was one particular topic that found itself being the primary aspiration in the household. My parents have been the perfect example of this statement. As far as I can remember, my parents have always been open to learning. My father is a well-educated man who is always eager to read and learn, who has traveled and participated in many conferences and formations where he acquired new skills and information with the aim of being an asset in his profession and his community. My mother is a devoted nurse who has offered her assistance to her community for almost thirty years now. She is as well very keen to partake in seminars and classes that train and educate on the latest care and treatments for her patients. My parents could not have been more specific and clear as to emphasizing the importance of education.

Coming from a third world country, it is essential for one to attain as much knowledge as possible in order to live an honest life. Sometimes, even with the expertise, it is a struggle to realize such objective.

I have heard many say, "Why go to school? Bill Gates did not graduate from college, and look what he had accomplished." Such mind-set is alarming, and it saddens me whenever I hear such statement. For starters, you are not Bill Gates, and his life is not yours. Never base judgments simply on what you see in someone's life. Without passion and goals, Bill Gates would not have achieved so much. I believe the reason for such way of thinking is we do not fully understand the importance of education. It is made to be believed in this world that without an education, you are nothing. Thus, many go to school to answer to the standards of society, not for self-accomplishment.

I never was one who loved school growing up. I was not a straight A student, and I struggled to pass my classes. I have a younger sister who, on the other hand, is very intelligent, and I felt like I had to keep up with her. Being a year apart did not help, for it was a constant pressure. I would spend sleepless nights studying, cramming information, crying, and not understanding why I could not score as high as she did. Although my parents never made me feel less of a person, I forced myself to believe that I was not as intelligent as she was. Throughout the years, I had to learn that everyone has his or her own talents and potentials. That is what makes us UNIQUE. There is only one: Amanda Exantus. I had to teach myself to be content with the person that I am. As long as I give my all and put a lot of effort in whatever the task may be, the result will reflect on what I have invested.

It breaks my heart whenever I see my fellow companions waste such opportunity for foolish reasons. Some of you picture these four upcoming years of college as the only time in life you will get to explore without holding back. You watch these movies that portray this time as one you will never forget, and you anticipate for *the* day—the day you will get to leave home, your parents, and siblings and enter the independent life. Unfortunately, these movies fail to mention many things such as financial struggles, pressure, depression, deadlines, responsibilities, breakups, relationship issues, and many more. I do not want to come off as the girl who is bashing everyone who goes out, socializes, and makes the best out of their college years. This season in your life is indeed one where you get to meet people from all over the world and experience a whole new side of life. Yet I want you all to remember the number one reason why you applied to go to college, and that is to amplify your knowledge in order to be successful in your chosen career. Why can't we have the best of both worlds?

I added more pressure on myself than even my parents did. I took it as my responsibility to do my best and take full advantage of this opportunity. I was aware of the sacrifices that came with my being here, and I wanted to allow myself to perform to the best of my abilities. Attending a private university, where as an international student I was not eligible for any financial aid, made me see things differently. I did face days when I got lazy and did not want to do any homework or days when I was satisfied with a lousy C on an assignment. Throughout my college experience, I have made mistakes and struggled. Nothing in life comes easy. One of my religion teachers, Dr. De Alminana, stated, "Freshmen are like fresh meats, we come in the situation only seeing the positive and exciting parts of college. As we move on to our sophomore years, we become wise morons, for we now realize that it is not always peachy and sweet. As juniors and seniors, we are now fully experiencing life as we are preparing ourselves to head out in the real world. Things are becoming more real and less cool."

It blows my mind whenever I hear stories of individuals from back home who come to the States or anywhere overseas for their education yet misuse their tuition money to buy cars, go out, and spend it on foolish things, leaving their parents defeated, inconsolable, and hopeless. You are now about to enter college; let this be your focus as you devote yourself to such commitment. Some of you try to grow up too fast while others prolong their growing process. Either way, you are only harming yourself.

I got the opportunity to meet wonderful individuals in the past years, among them a girl who went beyond her ways to obtain her bachelor in premed. Despite the many obstacles she had to face, such as financial struggles, legal and psychological issues, and discouragement, she conquered and graduated. I felt blessed having the chance to share that day with her and see her walk on that podium filled with joy and pride as she reached for her diploma. I have a friend in the army who works and goes to school.

When he is not in training, he is working from 8:00 p.m. till 4:00 a.m. and has to get up early to attend his classes at noon. I recently celebrated with a friend who graduated this fall, and it was an awesome day. She faced so many trials. From being kicked out of her dorm for financial issues, having to visit the financial aid office every semester of her four years of college, to coming up with some type of payment plan, she accomplished her goal. A few hours before graduation, she managed to clear out her balance and proudly walked to get her diploma. I am encouraged and blessed when I witness these stories, for they are reminders that it is possible. There will be a lot of bumps along the way; this is why it is crucial that one chooses his or her field wisely, for their passion will be their motivation when faced with these tough times.

Now, some might say that college is not for them. I can understand, for not everyone can afford or is qualified to attend college. Yet it is important that you undertake the proper approaches in specializing and investing in the areas you are good at and love (such as hair, nails, technology, cars, designing, singing, writing, painting, dancing, cooking, hosting, acting, and many more). To excel in something, you have to obtain as much understanding and techniques as possible in order to become an expert. We tend to minimize the careers we judge are not demanding or important as others. We usually see this in athletics, where many argue that gymnastic, for example, is not a sport. They tend to look past the hours of training, exercising, and learning in order to master the flips, jumps, and balance. Some do the same when it comes to singing; however, they are clueless of the work that goes into it.

Recognizing how blessed and privileged you are is essential when enrolling in college or any type of school, for it will change the way you go about a lot of things. Many long to be in your position but are unable to do so for multiple reasons. It is no longer about pleasing your parents with good grades and passing your classes but to set your education as your number one priority and personal achievement.

I cannot stress enough on the importance of education. Everyone has goals and objectives in life, and they differ from one person to another. My belief is that education is the main element to the realization of these goals. You will not only be more equipped to thrive in life; also you will be rewarding yourself.

THE BEST DECISION

Not everything comes along just when you want it. There are times when choices just have to be made or you'll simply miss out.

—Frances McDormand,

Miss Pettigrew Lives for a Day, 2008

AS CHILDREN, WE tend to dream big and float on clouds when we are asked this question, "Who do you want to be when you grow up?" From wanting to become a cowboy, a superhero, an astronaut, a scientist, a detective, to being the president of our countries, we have great ambitions. However, somewhere along the line of aging, we lose that fire and settle for average. Growing up, I wanted to be a teacher, a singer, a dancer, an artist, a designer, a stylist, a writer, a psychologist . . . And the list goes on. I used to be made fun of when I would write my

little romance novels, but my mom and my auntie Tatie Mare would always encourage me and proofread my books. Of course, as you are maturing, you start narrowing your list down to the few things you are most passionate about.

After many years in school, learning, building friendships, and discovering your inner self, you feel prepared to take the next step in your life. So you think! Most would consider such step to be graduating from high school and pursuing advanced education in the selected profession they feel called to. Having such importance, the answer to the question, "Who do you want to be when you grow up?" has been taken, unfortunately, too lightly.

One area in which most schools in my country lack is "guidance to the future." Most students find themselves in their last year of high school still wondering what they want to do. One of the many reasons why they are facing such trouble can be because they are unaware of their talents, who they are, what they are worth, and what their callings are. This does not necessarily mean everyone who is hesitant is clueless about who they are and what they want. I am addressing to those who have nothing to start off with, which makes graduating from high school look like one of the scariest chapters of their lives. From the numerous conversations I have had with fellow classmates, I always come across two common explanations to such ambiguity: parents and lack of opportunities.

Parents can be a justification to why children cannot come to a decision. Some undergo a lot of pressure or do not get the support needed from their parents. They either find themselves compromising or deviating from the career they were passionate about since they were youngsters.

I knew a guy who enrolled in premed as his major, not because he loved it, but as a result of his father pressuring him into this particular field. After failing his first year twice and taking a year off, he is now in the States still striving to become a doctor. There might be different reasons why he cannot succeed. One can be because he is not applying himself enough, and his father, knowing his potential, pushes him to live up to his capabilities. Another can be because he does not know himself well enough to realize

AMANDA EXANTUS

that such field is not for him. Everyone is capable, yet not everyone is called to be in a particular field, thus the reason why there are those who are doctors, others engineers, accountants, realtors, entrepreneurs, psychologists, teachers, writers, singers, artists, and so on. In other words, we can be whoever we want to be; however, you cannot force anyone to become something they are not and expect them to perform their best.

Since she was a little girl, my sister knew she was called to be a pediatrician. She loves children and shares that special bond with them that is indescribable. I remember in high school, she would be surrounded by the elementary children who knew her by name. She would embrace them and care for them. She is getting ready to graduate this April as a premed undergrad, which is a step less into becoming one of the finest pediatrician.

Psychology has been a subject that always intrigued me and I was very curious to explore. My last year in high school was my favorite, for I had a psych class, which only augmented my interest in the matter. When it came time for me to choose what my major was going to be, psychology was the first on my list. However, my father was hesitant about my choice and explained to me how such profession was not yet well perceived in Haiti. If I were to become a psychologist at that time, I would struggle financially, professionally, emotionally, and mentally before rising and blossoming in my career.

It is important to seek advice and wisdom from your elders when it comes to making such essential decisions, for they are well experienced and were once in your position. It does not mean you have to do as they say, yet you have a broader view on how to go about when making your final decision.

My father's analysis was correct. In Haiti, psychology is not well embraced, and people do not yet understand the importance of the science. After many deliberations, I selected business management as my major, yet the passion for psychology was still existent. I enrolled in Southeastern University and was determined to take full advantage of the opportunities by adding psychology as my minor. As for longtime goals, slowly but surely, I plan on continuing my studies till I obtain my doctorate in psychology. Although I did not start off with my main choice, I could not be more content, for I get to study people's behavior on a larger scale (in the business area).

It is important to always follow your heart, for you will never be satisfied until you are doing what you love. I know that I am called to be a psychologist, yet there is a reason why I am acquiring all these knowledge also in the business field. Sometimes we limit ourselves to certain things when we are capable of more. I have a heart for people, and adding management skills to the package can only strengthen the end result. I used to joke around and say after completing my bachelor in management that I would give the diploma to my father. Today I am glad that I can now see the bigger picture, and how much of an asset it will be as I mesh these two fields together. I am grateful for my father's input in my decision.

Another aspect that can play a role in this hesitancy is the limitation one might face, especially in an underdeveloped country. The professions, which tend to guarantee a stable living (according to society) are those in the medical field, law, business, engineering, entrepreneurship, banking, economics, accounting, management, etc. There are so many talents in my country that are being wasted or undiscovered, because society decides what makes one somebody. There is also that mind-set where if you practice certain occupations (such as being a teacher, a psychologist, a sociologist, a nurse, an assistant, a musician, a dancer, a painter, an artist, a stylist, etc.), the chances of success are slim. Such mentality only restricts the development of the communities, for it takes all sorts to generate a well-functioning country. It is really hard to shine in some careers, for you have to fight to earn a living and respect. It is important to understand why getting an education and choosing the right major are some of the most important decisions you will have to make in your life, for it will define your future.

As you are planning for tomorrow, you want to be excited when you wake up in the morning to go to work, looking forward to interacting with your coworkers, being productive, and being a positive feature to your community. No matter what it is you choose to specialize in, it is essential that you are passionate about it. It is certain that everything will not be handed to you on a silver platter, yet it is your responsibility to make sure that you know where you want to go and do your best to get there.

"Guidance to the future" can be a program where students who find themselves in great difficulty of making such decision could enroll in and get proper guidance to the right choice. I believe by doing so, unpleasant outcomes such as wasting money, depression, confusion, and dropouts can be prevented. I can relate to those who feel torn between being realistic and following their hearts; however, it is not an impossible decision. With guidance and support, the right choice will be made, and success will follow.

THE SELF

The man who views the world at fifty the same as he did at twenty has wasted thirty years of his life.

—Muhammad Ali

Man cannot remake himself without suffering, for he is both the marble and the sculptor.

—Dr. Alexis Carrel

THIS PARTICULAR SUBJECT is one many misconstrue and struggle with. Can you ever know yourself completely? Can you ever see yourself as others see you? Life is a daily battle; from the moment you wake up and step out of the door, you are heading toward several obstacles that you are called to face and conquer. The approach is not always as easy as we observe in other people's lives; however, they are possible to surmount. I have whined, cried, failed, gave up, overcame, and conquered difficulties so far in my life, and it is only the beginning. The positive thing about it all is with these hard times come wisdom and maturity.

I have tried to analyze and better myself by frequently searching from within and taking into account the changes I have experienced. As Dr. Alexis Carrel stated "The different experiences we face open doors for reflection." Through the betrayal of friends, the ending of a long-term relationship, and being away from my family, I had to remake myself, learn who I am, and search for the woman I was called to be all along. The areas I have observed many wrestle with are appearance and identity.

Appearance

Who decides what beauty is or looks like? Who has the right to say what your complexion, your eyes, your face, your body, the length of your hair, your height, your shape, your style, your nails, or your voice should look or sound like. Under what qualifications does one get to be voted the number one gorgeous woman in the world? According to *People* magazine, in 2011 Jennifer Lopez got the title of the most beautiful woman in the world. Yet many protest when young girls are starving, cutting themselves, or having unnecessary surgeries. It is mind-blowing listening to people ask these questions when the problem is all around them. It is interesting because I find myself sometimes among these girls who struggle.

For years, I have struggled with acne, and you would think it ameliorates with age; unfortunately, it is an ongoing and present issue. It is such a sensitive topic for me. I try my best to not talk about it, but whenever I do, it is because I cannot handle the thoughts by myself anymore. I have tried most of the products out there, and some would not work while others would but only for a period. There are days where I just call my mom and break down, and nights where I would cry myself to sleep.

I personally do not like makeup, yet I found myself purchasing foundations and powder in order to cover the blemishes and hide what I judged to be ugly. There were times where no concealer could hide my dark spots. Some days I refused to look at myself in the mirror for I was repulsed by what I saw. It was something I needed to overcome, for it was so toxic. Once the thoughts are there, everything inside of you change. You drag everything and everyone down with you. No matter what people around you might say or try, it is meaningless, for you are not willing to listen and accept. My mom had repeatedly tried her best to comfort me, and some days she brought me relief while other days there was nothing that she could say or do to console me. One thing that my friends and even family members did not understand was that I was not looking for praises or compliments, for as they affirmed them, I did not see what they saw.

I felt so misunderstood, for no loved ones of mine had to struggle with such nuisance for the amount of years that I have. I have no one whom I could really relate to. My self-esteem has been shattered as a result of this matter. I have missed many events, for I judged I was not presentable enough to attend. I have lied on the reasons why I was unable to go out with friends and share memories. This situation is as dangerous as any detrimental issues others face, for it numbs you to the core and affects other areas in your life.

I was advised to try and talk to a counselor that could help me get rid of these thoughts. I thought about it but felt if I wanted to be able to look at myself in the mirror one day and love what I see, it would have to come from me.

I love to smile. I was told a simple smile can change someone's day; this is why I take pleasure in smiling all the time. Seeing how a smile can bring so much light into someone else's life, I thought why not try it on myself? I woke up one day and starred in the mirror; not really liking what I saw, I smiled. I might have to dig deeper than others or go beyond measures to see what they see; the important thing is I found it. I will never look like Jennifer Lopez; nevertheless, I am a beautiful woman with a gorgeous smile and eyes that get smaller when I smile.

As of today, I still struggle with my acne and have days where I wake up and cry or do not like what I see. Yet I am taking the proper steps I need to overcome the situation. It is not about what others see but what I need to see when I look at myself. It does not matter the number of times you are told how pretty you are; if you do not see it, then the compliments are worthless. Most importantly, I remind myself constantly that I am a daughter of the Heavenly Father who created me in His image, and that enough should say it all. We are beautiful, for we are God's chef d'oeuvre, and everything that God creates is good and beautiful. Although we have days where we fail to remember those words of encouragement, I am here today to remind you.

Identity

As culture and society change and evolve, so do we humans. Can you imagine being the same little girl or boy you were fifteen years ago? We were created to grow and mature as we develop. It is important to have an idea of who you are as you enter any situation, especially going away to college. The idea of meeting new people and rooming with someone you barely know can be exciting and overwhelming at the same time. The simplest things—from identifying whether or not you are a morning or night person, the things you can and cannot tolerate, and your level of cleanliness, to your values and morals—are important to know about yourself. Many leave for college to experience different things, and being around a certain environment can shift your priorities as you get influenced by your peers.

I enrolled into a Christian school as a foreign student with a Catholic background. It took me a while to adjust, for I felt so out of place at times. There were days where I had never felt so offended by the different comments my peers and even teachers would make. I met an individual who, after knowing I was Catholic, stated, "My goal before you graduate is to convert you into a Christian." I was flabbergasted!

We worry so much about who is who that we lose focus at times. Attending this university was a blessing, for when I experienced the darkest moments of my life, I was in an environment that helped me rely on God, and I developed an awesome relationship with Him.

I have heard some say, "I was not given the chance to choose my religion, I was just born in it." It is an interesting comment. You cannot base your relationship with God on what your pastor or priest says, for we all have the free will to want to know of Him and His goodness. You may never fully agree with an individual's teaching; thus, it is for you to search God, seek His face and long for Him. Who am I? I am a daughter of my Heavenly Father, who entrusted me to my wonderful parents, who taught me about Him and His goodness. We worry so much about converting people into whomever, yet we miss our main purpose, which is to love one another and inform those who do not know about God and His love and mercy.

Who are you? No one can answer that question but you. Do not let anyone tell you who you are or speak any negativity into your life. Your surrounding may have called you worthless, dumb, bum, a nuisance, a mistake, a waste, yet the joys, pains, hurts, losses, gains, struggles, recoveries, restorations, achievements, failures, and opportunities you have known and will know in your life are the many elements that shape and will continue to transform you into becoming the man/woman you were created to be.

RELATIONSHIPS

Family

Families are the compasses that guide us. They are the inspiration to reach great heights, and our comfort when we occasionally falter.

—Brad Henry

N O MATTER HOW disconnecting or annoying they may seem to you, your parents are your support system. As you grow and begin to hit your teenage years, you are convinced that their goal is to prevent you from having a social life and enjoying yourself.

I used to find myself in this position where I thought my parents did not understand me or even tried. I used to complain about everything, for in my eyes, they were purposely contributing to my misery. Silly right? As dramatic as I sounded, yet with age and different experiences, I began to see through their eyes and hearts.

Believe it or not, parents are not here to torture you; on the contrary, they would do anything to keep you from any harm. We tend to forget that parents were once teens too; though the generations differ, the matters are somewhat similar. Guess what? At the end of the day, when everyone is gone, they are the ones who stand beside you. Some have probably heard this too many times, but from my experience, it has been the case. When you lose friends, boyfriends, or girlfriends or when all seems lost, your family will forever be there. I am sorry to tell you that it will not be that easy to get rid of them, and believe me, you do not want to. Sometimes it takes the tragedies of life, no matter how devastating and crucial they might be, to help one become aware of the many blessings he or she is surrounded by.

When I got on the plane from Port-au-Prince on January 10, 2010, never did I expect it would be the last time I would get to see some friends. The first minutes after the earthquake two days later, I got a call from my father informing me about the tragedy and assuring me that everyone was fine. I did not get too alarmed, for my dad sounded calm and safe. However, when I got back on campus and turned on the television, I became so cold and was overtaken by fear. The images were so graphic and disturbing that I could not help but to panic. I spent hours trying to call my parents but was unable to reach them. Facebook was the only source of communication between me and my friends from back home. Reading the names of those who were no longer alive was demoralizing. My friends whom I saw and hugged days before I left were no longer around. Never did I think while getting on that plane that it could be the last time that I might see my parents, my brother, my relatives, and my friends. Never did I think that my country, the one I built so many memories in, would never be the same. Two years later, I still have not gone home yet, and it has been challenging.

This incident has opened my eyes to realizing how blessed I am, and it has humbled me. It is so silly how sometimes we long for things that have always been in front of us but needed a situation to remind us or even open our eyes to the truth. I can say this tragedy did open my eyes and gave me an opportunity to develop a better relationship with my parents, to not take them for granted, and to actually appreciate them for who they are: amazing parents. It gave me an opportunity to appreciate my friends and, in return, be the best friend I can be. My lesson learned was to be more aware of the people around me, love those who love me, appreciate their role in my life, and not take them for granted.

There are certain situations or favors where you cannot count on anyone else but your family.

Growing up, I have watched my parents reach out to those in need. I have watched my aunts and uncles do the same by opening their homes, providing and going the extra mile for others. Last year, my uncle Jean drove my sister, my dad, and myself to Tallahassee, which is four hours away from his house, helped move and carry her belongings to the third floor of her apartment, and drove back to make it in time for work. On our way back, I was thanking him for such gesture, and I remember him saying, "There is no need to thank me. That is what family does." I am blessed and grateful for my family. Words will never be enough for me to express my gratitude toward my father, for I have seen him give his all for his children's well-being. He always encourages us to live to the best of our abilities and supports us in every dream and goal we have.

Again, it is not always peachy, especially within the family unit. Many of you cannot wait to go to college and get away from your family. I understand the need of wanting to experience new things and being on your own; however, never forget where you came from and who you are, and be mindful of your parent's sacrifices. I am sure that my parents would have loved to offer themselves nice gifts from time to time, go on vacation and cruises, travel the world. Yet their priorities are to provide and do their best (which sometimes include sleepless nights and sacrificing their needs) to offer us the best of this world.

Friendship

It's surprising how many persons go through life without ever recognizing that their feelings toward other people are largely determined by their feelings toward themselves, and if you're not comfortable within yourself, you can't be comfortable with others.

—Sidney J. Harris

"College is where you meet and make true friends who are going to be there throughout your lifetime." How true is this saying? Can it be classified as a myth? What would be the best way to describe the word *friend*?

I am currently in my last semester of undergrad, and I can say from my experience so far that college has definitely been an interesting season in my life. College is where you get the opportunity to meet all types of individuals from all around the world and also where you will expand your views on life and maybe alter your perception. As you turn the page to this new chapter in your life, being in a different environment away from your loved ones, you are called to rely on yourself and even others. You will gradually realize the numerous friends you will lose contact with, not as a result of conflicts, but simply because the relationships had no depth. Slowly as your list shrinks, you will begin to discover who the true friends were and are. Yet how can you be sure they are the true ones? Unfortunately, only time can tell; however, there are some clues.

For starters, life will throw obstacles at you, and whenever it does, look around. Those you do see might be the keepers. There are people you will meet in life that are only around to have fun and enjoy, but whenever things get hard, they are nowhere to be found. I remember watching one of Tyler Perry's plays where the character Madea was saying to her family, as I paraphrase, "Some people you meet are like leaves on a tree. As the wind blows away, so do they. There are others you meet who are like branches. A few blows do not carry them away, but eventually as they weaken, so do the friendship. Last but not least are the very few ones who are like the bark of a tree, where even through the most destructive wind, they are unbeatable." Friends are there for you and with you through the good and bad times. They may not have the answers to everything, but their shoulders are always there for you to lean on. It is also important to look at yourself and see the type of friend you are or have been to yours.

I asked what the definition of a friend is; here are some answers I got:

- Someone who cares for you, protects you, and supports you as we do for each other no matter distance. (Sebastien Jean)
- One who's willing to not only be there to laugh and have a good time but who is there when things aren't so pretty. A person who doesn't freak out when they see tears but who is right there with a warm hug, comforting words, tissues, and if that doesn't work, a big tub of ice cream. Someone whom you can trust with some of the most personal aspects of your life,

without ever feeling the slightest ounce of judgment. An individual who not only knows but embraces your flaws and still wants to kick it with you. One who encourages you yet isn't afraid to give you the truth even when it hurts. To me, that's a true friend. (Jessica James)

- I'm omnipresent . . . Always ready to do stuff for the person without limitation. (Olivier Boulin)

- Knows you, loves you, honors you, respects you, is there for you, cares for you, and prays for you . . . Something like that, lol. (Robert Aderno)

- If you can't respect the same sex, how do you expect to respect the opposite? Friendships are in fact preparation for marriage. (Nachombe Pierre)

One of the many things I have learned is you attract or are more likely to befriend individuals that are not too far from resembling yourself. What I mean is I believe the reason why you are friends with someone is because you share similar views, and they can vary from individuals.

Not all my friends are like me, and sometimes when I think about our personalities, it is hard for me to even understand how this friendship is even possible. Yet we love one another and have one another's best interest at heart. You cannot ask your friends to possess certain qualities that you yourself cannot replicate in return. We are so quick to blame others whenever a relationship does not work; sometimes we might have to look within ourselves and evaluate whether or not we are the reasons for these failures.

Fall semester of 2011, I was enrolled in a Management Information System class, and my teacher Mr. De Souza said one morning, "Love is patient, but do you give your loved ones time to grow?" It was interesting to hear, for I never reflected on my relationships from that angle. We are so quick to grow weary and throw in the towel when our friends do not see things as we do; however, we expect for others to show compassion toward us. When it comes to any type of relationship, it is about giving and receiving. It has to be reciprocal. No one wants to give without receiving the same treatment in return. Even when it comes to our

AMANDA EXANTUS

relationship with God, it is the same. All He asks of us is to obey His commandments and love one another, and He will bless us with everything else.

I have to say that the process of knowing who your real and true friends are can be draining and has many surprises that are not always pleasant. There will be times where you will be hurt, fighting to hold on to a seasonal friend, feeling alone or plainly confused. The main idea behind making a choice is selecting from within a list. There are situations where many feel they were not given the chance to choose, but life took the liberty to do so for them. However, the last thing you do not want to do is punish others as a result of previous experiences.

Bitterness is one of the worst feelings one can obtain, for it prevents you from living and enjoying the blessings that are in front of you. It is important to acquire wisdom as you overcome trials in life, for you do not want to repeat the same mistakes. As long as you are breathing and are living on this earth, you will be making mistakes and facing challenges when it comes to relationships; however, the main idea is to learn from them. Wisdom is acquired two ways, from your personal experiences and other people's experiences. The struggles of life are existent for a reason, and that is to build one's character.

One of the many things I have learned is the importance of knowing that God is always in control and works all things together for our good. I can assure you all that there will be times where inexplicable things will happen to you and you have no idea what is going on and why. What I have learned to do, though it is not always easy, is to rely on God, for He has our best interest at heart. He is a loving Father who would never let anything happen to his children. For I have dedicated my life to Christ to serve Him and live by His words, I trust and believe that God will see me through, for He has promised that he will *never* forsake me.

We were not placed on this earth to live alone, hence the reason why God created a man and a woman. No one said it was going to be easy, especially when it comes to dealing with individuals that are different from you. Yet in order to survive in this world, we are called to interact with others either at school, work, gatherings, events, or church. I have come to the conclusion that every relationship has for its foundation love, whether it is a friendship or an intimate relationship. The best definition of a friend, in my opinion, is in 1 Corinthian 13:4-7, "Love is patient and kind. Love is not jealous or boastful or proud [5] or rude. It does not demand its own way. It is not irritable, and it keeps no record of being wronged. [6] It does not rejoice about injustice but rejoices whenever the truth wins out. [7] Love never gives up, never loses faith, is always hopeful, and endures through every circumstance" (New Living Translation).

Of course no one is perfect; however, you can strive to live up to these words and be the best daughter/son, sister/brother, friend, wife/husband, and mother/father you can be to your loved ones.

BALANCE

There is a time for everything, and a season for every activity under heaven: A time to be born and a time to die, a time to plant and a time to uproot, a time to kill and a time to heal, a time to tear down and time to build, a time to weep and a time to laugh, a time to mourn and a time to dance, a time to scatter stones and a time to gather them, a time to embrace and a time refrain, a time to search and a time to give up, a time to keep and a time throw away, a time to tear and a time to mend, a time to be silent and a time to speak, and time to love and a time to hate, a time for war and a time for peace.

—Ecclesiastes 3:1-8

I GREW UP hearing this French saying, "L'excès en tout nuit," which I could translate as, "Too much of anything is a bad thing." We sometimes rush into situations for various reasons, which, from my observations, some can be caused by fabricated truth, fear, pressure, circumstances of life, etc. I believe our environment can also be groundwork for such rush. My mother used to always tell me, "There is a time for everything in life, do not force things." It took me a while to fully grasp and understand it, for there were times when I wanted to live an experience and did not understand my parents' disapprovals (for example, I remember when I was in high school and wanted to go party with my friends or wanted to date). Do not try to juggle too much at once, for everything will fall into place as you let them occur at their own pace. Do not feel forced or obliged to undertake certain actions only because it is the norm.

Setting priorities can help manage the different tasks of life, for it develops a level of determination and discipline one needs to own in order to accomplish set goals. There are things that are more important than others; it is for you to evaluate, weigh, and select those that are significant to you. Not everything is possible to complete with your own strength or in your own timing; thus, you go on not understanding how you cannot achieve or enjoy certain things. As you rush situations in your life to take place, the more you feel the shift from the lack of balance.

As a college student, it can be hard to adjust to a new surrounding and try to fully live the college experience yet excel academically. I have seen students get jobs in their freshman year and struggle to pass their classes. I have also noticed others who, not by choice, had to get a job and managed to balance things perfectly. Only you know how much you can handle and your ability to perform well. Be wise when it comes to making such decision. Some might have to take a semester off in order to collect enough money for their tuition while others might have to take fewer classes. Few might have to choose between not working and focusing on their classes or taking a few semesters off and securing their tuition funds. Not everybody has the same abilities; thus, it is important to know yours.

The main question is then, How do you balance everything in life without getting overwhelmed with day-to-day life circumstances? I personally think a lot goes into finding out an answer to this matter; however, I think it is fair to say that discipline should have its place in the list. As duties and responsibilities become more defined, the more complicated and harder it gets to stabilize each area in your life. Professor De Souza used to always say, "You guys, I promise you, once your relationship with God is great, your relationship with others and everything else will balance just right."

I took the liberty of posting the question asked earlier on my Facebook wall, and these were the answers I got:

- For me, personally coming to the realization that there will always be something in life that I just can't control helps to level the playing field in the sense that it helps me to prioritize the different things in my life. Taking more time to work on things that I can fix and relying on Christ to deal with the things/circumstances that are out of my control. Remembering that life is a compilation of seasons helps a lot too! I try to take it a couple of hours at a time on GOOD days. That way I don't get frustrated and overwhelmed . . . And on NOT so good days, literally minute by minute. It helps to understand that everything happens for a reason, and I thus try to find the good in all things. But hey, let's be real I'm not gonna walk around with a fake smile plastered on my face when things aren't going great. And it's during times like that when I look to Christ to lean on, the one individual who will either directly give me the supernatural strength to pull through or indirectly send people my way to walk along side of me and help me out. (Jessica James)

- To me it is having a sense of God peace surrounding the mind, heart, and environment:) also filling in the mind with His truth which gives the sense of peace that things are going to be okay. (Emmanuella Augusme)

- I would personally say take everything step by step and day by day. Find out what works for you and stick with it . . . Don't be afraid to ask for help when needed! Make time to do something you totally enjoy and would do every day if you had the chance. Find your weaknesses and turn them into strengths and make your strengths even stronger. Surround yourself with people with wisdom and would give you godly advice. And most importantly, ask God for guidance, discipline, courage, humility and let him be the one that leads you each day. (Ruth Mezamour)

I do not have the answers to every problem you will face as you are getting ready to enroll into this new season of your life. I am as well learning each day. There are situations that are beyond our capabilities to handle or solve, and as we face them, it is wise that we lean on the one and only, to whom nothing is impossible, and that is God. I have found myself in situations where I had to let go of people, and it took a supernatural strength to open my fists. I had to forgive people who did me wrong where if it were up to me, they would have never been forgiven. There is a time to mourn and a time to rejoice. How do you ever get past the grieving part, to ever get to rejoice after losing a loved one?

Sometimes we find ourselves struggling to balance things in our lives because we are too focused trying to walk on a thin line with both our hands and head filled with baggage. We can be greedy at times where we want to handle everything all at once. The overall lesson I have learned when it comes to balancing things around me and in my life is that some things are beyond my control, and my attitude toward these situations are crucial.

I believe the way you can live a balanced life is with serenity, and this short prayer says it all: "God grant me the serenity to accept the things I cannot change, courage to change the things I can, and the wisdom to know the difference."

REFERENCES

Ali, Muhammad. *http://www.quotegarden.com/self-discovery.html*.

Carrel, Dr. Alexis. *http://www.quotegarden.com/self-discovery.html*.

Edelman, Marian Wright. *http://www.great-inspirational-quotes.com/education-quotes.html*.

Harris, Sidney J. *http://www.great-inspirational-quotes.com/relationship-quotes.html*.

Henry, Brad. *http://www.great-inspirational-quotes.com/family-quotes.html*.

Kaufman, Bel. *http://www.great-inspirational-quotes.com/education-quotes.html*.

McDormand, Frances. *http://www.reellifewisdom.com/taxonomy/term/decision_making?page=1*.

INDEX

A

Aderno, Robert, 47

ambitions, 22–24

  parents as factors in
achieving, 24–26

  societal limitations in
achieving, 27–28

Augusme, Emmanuella, 56

B

bitterness, 49

Boulin, Olivier, 47

C

college, 44

  alternatives of, 19

  expectations of, 16

  hardworking students in,
18–19, 54

  preparations for, 18, 20,
26–28, 36, 57

  reason for going to, 16–17

  student experiences in, 54

D

De Alminana (college
religion teacher), 17

De Souza (MIS teacher), 48